About Prayer

Les Miller

NOVALIS

Cover design: Mardigrafe
Cover illustration: Anna Payne-Krzyzanowski
Interior images: Jupiter Images: p. 31; Plaisted: p. 5; WP Wittman: pp. 16, 19, 23, 25, 35, 43
Layout: Mardigrafe and Audrey Wells
Reviewed by Heather Reid

Published by Novalis

Publishing Office
10 Lower Spadina Avenue, Suite 400
Toronto, Ontario, Canada
M5V 2Z2

Head Office
4475 Frontenac Street
Montréal, Québec, Canada
H2H 2S2
www.novalis.ca

Library and Archives Canada Cataloguing in Publication

Miller, Les, 1952-
25 questions about prayer / Les Miller.

Issued also in an electronic format.

ISBN 978-2-89646-376-3

1. Prayer--Juvenile literature. I. Title. II. Title: Twenty-five questions about prayer.

BV212.M55 2011 j248.3'2 C2011-904230-4

Printed in Canada.

We acknowledge the financial support of the Government of Canada through the Canada Book Fund for business development activities.

5 4 3 2 1 15 14 13 12 11

TABLE OF CONTENTS

A WORD FROM THE AUTHOR.. 5

DEEPENING OUR FRIENDSHIP WITH GOD 6

1. What is prayer? 6
2. Why should I pray? 7
3. What are some different types of prayer? 9
4. How often should I pray? 10
5. How do I pray? 12
6. What do the scriptures tell us about prayer? 14
7. How did Jesus pray? 15

COMMON PRAYERS OF THE CHURCH 17

8. Why is the Our Father or Lord's Prayer important? ... 17
9. Why do we pray to Mary? 18
10. What is a litany? 20
11. What is the Liturgy of the Hours? 21
12. Why do we say Grace when we eat? 22
13. Why do some people put their hands together or kneel when they pray? 24
14. What special prayers do we use when someone dies? 26
15. Why do we end our prayers with "Amen"? 27

PERSONAL WAYS OF PRAYING 28
16. Can we use our own words when we pray?............. 28
17. Is singing hymns a form of prayer? 29
18. How can reading be prayer? 31
19. How can writing be prayer? 32
20. How can creating something be prayer? 34
21. Why is silence an important part of prayer? 36

CHALLENGES TO PRAYER 38
22. Why do we memorize certain prayers? 38
23. Do we pray to change God's mind? 39
24. Does God always answer our prayers? 41
25. How does prayer help the world? 42

WORDS TO KNOW 44

PRAYERS TO LEARN BY HEART 46

A Word from the Author

Jesus spent only a few short years teaching and healing. During this time, he told people of God's love for them. No job has ever been or ever will be as important as that one, and yet Jesus often set aside time to pray. Sometimes he prayed with his disciples and other followers, and sometimes he prayed alone. Sometimes he used formal prayers, and sometimes he talked to God in his own words. Often he prayed in silence.

Jesus is our greatest model for living as Christians. If we want to follow in his footsteps, we need to pray.

Our prayer life is incredibly important. Prayer keeps us in touch with God and gives us strength, peace and hope to do our daily tasks. Prayer also deepens our friendship with God. As with any friend, we need to speak and listen to God to have a good relationship. The more often we communicate, the stronger the friendship will be. But God is much more than a friend. God brings meaning and happiness into our lives.

When we are busy, it is easy to think we don't have time for prayer. We have so many other things to do! We often tell ourselves we will pray later. Or maybe we don't feel sure of ourselves when we pray. Am I praying correctly? we may wonder. Are there other ways of praying that would be better?

This book talks about reasons for praying and describes different types of prayer. It also explores challenges you might have when you pray. My prayer for you is that this book will draw you into a deeper relationship with God by leading you to spend more time with God in prayer.

Les Miller

1

What is prayer?

Prayer is communication with God. When we talk with someone, we listen to them and they listen to us. We do the same thing in prayer. We use thoughts or words to talk to God and we use silence to listen for God's response. Most prayers begin by addressing God, just as we use a person's name when we speak to them.

The aim of prayer is to grow closer to God and to feel that God is very close to us. Although it is hard to put it into words, the peace and warmth we feel at these times comes from God's love and friendship. We may respond to these moments by giving thanks for God. At other times, God doesn't seem very near to us. Our prayer then becomes one of searching and longing. We may tell God that we feel distant and out of touch with what is sacred or holy. During these moments, we need to be quiet so we can hear God speaking to us.

Some kinds of prayer are best said on our own, while some kinds are best done with other people. When we pray together, we meet God in a special way. Jesus said, "Where two or three are gathered in my name, I am there among them." (Matthew 18:20) Praying together brings families, classes and parish communities closer together. We use the same words and we sing the same songs. This shows that we belong together as Christians. Often we use traditional prayers, such as Grace before meals or the Lord's Prayer (Our Father). But we can also pray in our own words, from the heart. In this way we communicate our own needs and feelings and take time to deepen our awareness of what God is telling us.

- Prayer is different from other sacred words. Prayer is direct communication with God.

- All major world religions include prayer as a key part of their practices. Many Hindus and Buddhists practise meditation. In meditation, the person tries to be still and listen to God speaking to them in their hearts. Some Christian prayers come from prayers of the Jewish tradition.

2

Why should I pray?

All our relationships, with family and friends, need time and care if they are to grow. It would be hard to feel close to someone if you never talk to them or hear from them. Over time, you would feel less and less connected to them.

It's not that different when we talk about connecting with God. When we pray, we "hang out" with God. The more we are aware of God's presence in all we do, the closer we are to God. That's why it helps to have reminders of God in your everyday life, such as wearing a cross around your neck, saying Grace before meals, or saying a prayer of thanks before going to bed. Doing these things keeps our connection with God alive and strong.

Prayer helps us to become better people, because it calls us to see the world from God's point of view. God gives us messages of love, justice, joy and hope. If we listen to God when we pray, we can be more loving people. When we are close to God, it is harder to hurt others with our words and deeds.

It is also our duty to pray. Jesus asks us to pray, gives us words for prayer and shows us how to pray.. The Church asks that we pray each day to keep our relationship with God strong. When we get distracted or caught up in what we're doing, the discipline of prayer helps us. It reminds us to open our hearts to God in our busy lives.

Goodbye is a short form of *God be with you*. Every time we say it, we are *blessing* the other person!

3

What are some different types of prayer?

There are as many forms of prayer as there are ways of communicating. We can sense God's presence in countless ways. For example, we can see God in the beauty of creation and in the *sacraments*, particularly in the Body of Christ at Mass. Also, we can hear God's word being spoken to us when someone reads aloud from the Bible.

We can look at these many types of prayer according to what we are doing when we pray:

- **Blessing and adoration:** We know that God loves us very deeply. Prayers of *blessing* and *adoration* say that we also love God very much.
- **Petition and intercession:** For some of our needs and hopes, only God can help us. We describe these desires in *prayers of petition*. In these prayers we also ask God to forgive our wrongdoings. Above all, we ask for God's love to guide the hearts and minds of all people on earth. In *prayers of intercession*, we ask God to help certain people or situations in need of God's care.
- **Thanksgiving:** In these prayers, we recognize the many gifts God has given us.

- **Praise:** In prayers of praise, we praise God's greatness and majesty.

How do we decide which way to pray? It depends on what is happening in our lives. If we climb a mountain or hike through the woods on a beautiful day, we might praise God, the creator of all. If we are going through a hard time, we might ask God to help us. In prayer, we can say whatever is in our hearts or on our minds.

When we pray for others, we should also include our enemies. That's what Jesus told us to do.

The Mass includes all these forms of prayer. *Eucharist*, another word we use for Mass, means *thanksgiving*.

4

How often should I pray?

Some religions call for believers to pray a certain number of times each day. Christians do not follow this kind of strict rule, but St. Paul says that we should pray continually. (1 Thessalonians 5:17) He does not mean we should be on our knees talking to God 24 hours a day, but that everything we do could be a way of praying to God. For example, if we are in school and we are trying to learn, we are telling God through our actions that we want to grow and be the best we can be.

Whenever we pray, we need to give it our full attention. Many Catholics like to spend a few minutes praying when they get up in the morning, before they eat (by saying Grace), as they begin work or school, and before they go to sleep at night. Going to Mass or praying the Rosary are two other important ways to pray for Catholics. (See *25 Questions about Catholic Signs and Symbols* for a full explanation of the Rosary.)

As we will see in Question 11, priests and religious sisters and brothers pray at set times of the day. It is comforting to know that throughout the world, someone is praying for the Church (that's us!) all the time.

Muslims pray five times a day. They have special body positions for the various prayers. Because they must pray on a clean surface, many Muslims carry prayer mats to place on the floor or ground during prayer. They pray with their bodies facing the Saudi Arabian city of Mecca, which is the most holy place for Muslims.

Some Jewish people pray three times a day. They may pray wearing a special prayer shawl called a *tallit*. Some also wear tiny boxes strapped to their foreheads and on their arms, next to their hearts. The boxes contain a passage from scripture that God asked them to keep close to their minds and hearts.

5

How do I pray?

As we have seen, prayer is all about turning our hearts and minds to God. There are many different paths to prayer. You need to find the ways that work for you. Wisdom from holy people through the ages may be helpful here.

When St. Benedict founded his monastery at Monte Cassino, Italy, he set specific times for the monks to pray. While we may not have the same schedule as monks, some specific times of day may work well for us. What time of day is best for you to pray? Maybe it is when you get up or come home from school. It could be in the evening with your family around the dinner table or just before you go to bed. Finding a regular time and place is a key way to make prayer an important part of your life.

You can use traditional prayers, such as the Our Father or Lord's Prayer. (See the prayers at the end of this book for some more examples.) You can pray in your own words or through your actions. Sometimes just by sitting still for a little while we can discover that God is trying to communicate with us.

No matter which style of prayer you try, keep these few simple points in mind to help you pray:

- Make sure you have enough time for prayer. If you are thinking about another place you need to be, you will be distracted and your prayer will not be as deep as it could be.
- Pick a time of day that's good for you.
- Pray in a place where you won't be disturbed, where you are comfortable, and where you have everything you might need (such as a Bible, prayer book or journal: see Question 19 for more about using a journal for prayer).

St. Ignatius of Loyola wrote a beautiful prayer for early morning, when we are looking forward to the day. It begins, "Father, I dedicate this new day to you; as I go about my work, I ask you to bless those with whom I come in contact."

St. Thérèse of Lisieux wrote, "For me prayer is an upward leap of the heart, an untroubled glance toward heaven, a cry of gratitude and love which I utter from the depths of sorrow as well as from the heights of joy."

6

What do the scriptures tell us about prayer?

The Old and New Testaments (the two parts of the Bible) offer wisdom about praying.

- Abraham (in the Old Testament) showed both faithfulness and courage in his prayer. He prayed to God for the souls of sinful people in a series of prayers of petition.
- Moses met God in several powerful ways. The prayer of Moses was for strength to lead the Israelites out of Egypt. We read in Exodus (in the Old Testament) that Moses talked for a long time with God, as if talking to a friend. We long for this friendship with God in our prayer.
- The Psalms (in the Old Testament) are 150 prayers that are still prayed today in Jewish and Christian worship. They describe Israel's love for God and God's love for God's people.
- The *Magnificat*, the beautiful prayer that Mary prayed when she reflected on becoming the mother of Jesus, is a model for Christian life. It is full of joy, praise, courage, trust, hope and wisdom.
- In the Acts of the Apostles (in the New Testament), the early Church followed the teachings of Jesus by praying together as a community inspired by the Holy Spirit.

- St. Paul's letters (in the New Testament) show how we can pray for others in blessing and thanksgiving. For example, he wrote to the people of Philippi, "I thank my God every time I remember you, constantly praying with joy in every one of my prayers for all of you, because of your sharing in the gospel from the first day until now." (Philippians 1:3)

We read in the Bible about people using different positions for prayer. Some kneeled (1 Kings 8:45), bowed (Exodus 4:31) or stood (1 Kings 8:22), while others fell on their faces (2 Chronicles 20:18; Matthew 26:39). See Question 13 for more about positions we can use for praying.

7

How did Jesus pray?

Jesus would have learned to pray from his parents, Mary and Joseph. They would have taught him traditional Jewish prayers and the importance of having a close relationship with God. It was the growing awareness of the depth of his relationship with God, his "*Abba*" or Father, that led Jesus into his deepest prayer. His oneness with God helped Jesus to see himself as the Son of God.

At the beginning of his ministry, Jesus went alone into the desert to pray. The desert is a place of great simplicity and few distractions. The spiritual strength that came from his prayer allowed him to keep following God's will for him, even though he was tempted to give up. Later in his ministry, Jesus would find quiet places to pray, such as a lake or a mountaintop.

In moments of joy and triumph, Jesus prayed words of thanksgiving and adoration. He encourages us to pray deeply, joyfully and continuously. He also gave us a beautiful prayer as a way of reaching out to God: the Our Father or Lord's Prayer. (We'll explore that prayer in the next question.) At the Last Supper with his disciples, Jesus prayed to God. On the cross and in pain, he found words from the *Psalms* to express his sorrow.

Jesus not only shows us how to pray, he also brings our prayers to God. This is why we often end our prayers "through Jesus Christ our Lord."

Although Jesus often prayed alone, he taught that praying together was very important, too. (See the Gospel according to Matthew, chapter 18, verses 19 to 20.)

8

Why is the Our Father or Lord's Prayer important?

During the Sermon on the Mount, Jesus told his disciples, "Pray then in this way: Our Father in heaven ..." (Matthew 6:9) The words that follow have become one of the best-known Christian prayers ever. Because it came to us from Jesus, it is often called the Lord's Prayer. We say it on our own and we say it together at Mass. (See the end of this book for the whole Lord's Prayer and learn it by heart if you don't already know it.) It is also one of the prayers of the Rosary.

This prayer also teaches us the main truths of the Gospel. After calling on God as Our Father, the prayer honours God's name, prays for the coming of God's kingdom of love, and asks for God's will to be done on earth and in heaven. We then ask God for help in dealing with our needs for food, forgiveness and safety from evil.

The words of the Lord's Prayer have rich meaning. Sometimes we may say the words as a routine, without focusing on what we are saying. It is a good practice to say the words slowly and think about the meaning of each phrase before moving on to the next one.

The Lord's Prayer unites Christians around the world in prayer. The languages they use may be different, but the meaning is the same.

- St. Thomas Aquinas, a great teacher in the Church, called the Lord's Prayer "the perfect prayer."
- A slightly shorter version of the Lord's Prayer is found in Luke's *Gospel* (Luke 10:2-4).

9

Why do we pray to Mary?

Mary is a very holy and blessed person. We sometimes ask her to guide us in our prayers and to bring them to God for us. Mary is a good guide for us because she gave birth to Jesus Christ, the Son of God. No human person is as close to Jesus as Mary is.

Mary also shows us the way to prayer through her own prayer life. Her beautiful prayer called the *Magnificat* (Luke 1:46-55) is filled with adoration, thanksgiving, joy, hope and trust. It reminds us that our prayer must be more than words: our hearts must also be turned to God with love.

Many Catholics feel very close to Mary and have a special love for her. She can't answer our prayers, for only God can do that. But she can help us on our path to holiness.

There are many prayers to Mary in the Catholic tradition. The best known is the Hail Mary. This is one of the prayers we pray when we pray the Rosary. (See the end of this book for the Hail Mary.) Other beautiful Marian prayers (prayers to Mary) include the *Memorare*, *Hail Holy Queen*, *Regina Caeli* and the *Angelus*.

When we pray to other holy people, such as saints, we are asking them to guide us and bring our prayers to God.

Traditionally, the Angelus is prayed three times a day, at 6:00 a.m., noon, and 6:00 p.m. This short prayer service includes the Hail Mary and Glory Be. In some cities we can still hear the Angelus bells calling people to pray this prayer.

10

What is a litany?

When we pray together as a community, we often pray in the form of a litany. A litany is a prayer of petition to God that goes back and forth between a leader, such as a priest, and the worshippers, who give the response. It may be spoken or sung. At Mass, there are several forms of litany, including the *Lamb of God* (Agnus Dei, in Latin) and the *Kyrie eleison* (Kir-ee-ay ay-lay-ee-zon):

The priest says, "Lord, have mercy."
We respond, "Lord, have mercy."

The priest says, "Christ, have mercy,"
We respond, "Christ, have mercy."

The priest concludes, "Lord, have mercy."
We respond, "Lord, have mercy."

Litanies began early in the Church's history. The *Kyrie* is perhaps the oldest Christian litany. (In Greek, *Kyrie eleison* means Lord, have mercy, and *Christe eleison* means Christ, have mercy.) In the early Church in Rome, worshippers would recite different litanies as they moved from one holy place to another.

Other litanies developed over time. Today, one of the most beloved litanies is the Litany of the Saints. In this litany, many saints are named by the leader. We ask each saint to pray to God for our needs when we respond, "Pray for us." In this litany, we also pray directly to God through Jesus and the Holy Spirit.

- The word "litany" comes from an ancient Greek word, *litaneia*, which means a fervent prayer request.
- The Church encourages worshippers to participate as fully, as consciously and as actively as possible in prayer and worship. Litanies offer us a way to do this.

11

What is the Liturgy of the Hours?

Many Catholics – Bishops, priests, deacons, religious sisters and brothers, and lay people – pray the Liturgy of the Hours several times every day. This prayer is being prayed by someone right now, somewhere in the world. It is so important that is also called the Prayer of the Church. Another name for it is the *Divine Office*. The words of the prayers are found in a book called a *breviary*. You can also find them on the Internet.

The Liturgy of the Hours has three major sets of prayers:

- early morning (the Office of Readings, or Matins)
- morning prayer (Lauds)
- evening prayer (Vespers).

Other (minor) prayer times are also observed. The Liturgy of the Hours is made up of some familiar prayers, the Psalms, brief passages from scripture, and intercessions.

Some monks and religious sisters observe a strict rule of praying the Liturgy of the Hours every three hours: midnight (Matins), dawn (Lauds), early morning (Prime), mid-morning (Terce), noon (Sext), mid-afternoon (None), evening (Vespers), and late evening (Compline). Today the Church suggests that praying in the morning and evening is a good practice for all Catholics.

12

Why do we say Grace when we eat?

Before sitting down to eat, many Catholics pray a short prayer called *Grace*. This word comes from the same root as the Italian word *grazie*, which means "thank you." In this prayer, we thank God for the gifts of food God gives us. It is also a prayer of blessing. We ask God to bless the food we are eating, the people at the table, those who are absent, those who helped prepare the meal, and those who do not have enough to eat.

Here is a well-known Grace:

Bless us, O Lord, and these your gifts,
which we are about to receive from your bounty.
Through Christ our Lord. Amen.

There are many other graces you can use. Look for some online and write out your favourites, then pray them with your family. (You may even find some graces that you can sing together.) Often the most powerful and heartfelt Grace is one that is in your own words. Take turns as a family saying a Grace before meals that comes straight from the heart.

Praying Grace before meals as a family reminds us that we belong to God and that our lives depend on God's gifts to us. It is only natural to give God thanks for all our blessings!

Grace before meals is only one example of family prayer. Here are a few others you can try:

- the Rosary (see *25 Questions about Catholic Signs and Symbols*)

- a morning prayer of consecration, where we dedicate our day to God
- a prayer at the end of the day
- special prayers in different liturgical seasons, such as Advent, when we light the candles of the Advent wreath to prepare for the birth of Jesus at Christmas.

Many cultures and traditions pray before meals. The Christian tradition of saying Grace was inherited from the Jewish people.

13

Why do some people put their hands together or kneel when they pray?

We use gestures to express our feelings and share our thoughts with other people. We smile to show we like something. We shake hands when we are introduced to someone. When we pray, besides using words, listening, writing or creating, we use physical gestures to tell God what we are thinking or feeling.

We often start with the Sign of the Cross. This helps us to remember that when we pray, we are praying to God. It also recognizes our belief in the Trinity: Father, Son and Holy Spirit.

Sometimes we put our hands together in prayer, with our fingers and palms together near our hearts. We are not sure how this practice began, but we know this gesture was used in ancient times when a servant wanted something from a master. Today it shows our relationship with God, our creator.

Sometimes we pray with our hands up and our arms outstretched. This is called the *orans* position and has been used for thousands of years. The priest uses this prayer position several times during Mass.

When we kneel to pray, we are saying that we are in awe of God's love, justice and power. In kneeling, we lower ourselves to show that we know God is greater than us and is to be honoured and adored. Kneeling is an ancient gesture of humility.

When we pray together, we often stand to pray. This is a sign of respect and praise. (Read more about this posture in *25 Questions About What We See in a Catholic Church.*)

Sometimes people show their humility in prayer by lying down on the ground, often in front of the altar. This is called *prostration.*

14

What special prayers do we use when someone dies?

When someone we love dies, we are full of sorrow. But we are not alone. We can turn to God in prayer to find comfort and meaning in these sad times. Familiar prayers can be a great help. They give us words when it is hard to express our feelings.

For example, we use the "Eternal Rest" prayer to ask for God's love and care for the person who has died:

Eternal rest grant unto them (him/her), O Lord,
and let perpetual light shine upon them (him/her).
May they (he/she) rest in peace. Amen.

We know that Mary suffered greatly when her son, Jesus, died. We join our sorrow to hers when we pray the Rosary. If you have been to a funeral home, you may have said the Rosary with other mourners.

Sometimes we pray Psalm 130, "Out of the depths." This prayer is over 2,500 years old. It speaks of the depths of our sorrow but also of our faith in God, who will guide us through hard times. It begins with these words:

Out of the depths I cry to you, O Lord.
Lord, hear my voice!
Let your ears be attentive

to the voice of my supplications!
(A supplication is a cry for help.)

Another psalm that is often associated with grief (but also with comfort and hope) is Psalm 23, "The Lord Is My Shepherd." This famous prayer talks about allowing God to lead us in dark times, like a shepherd leads his sheep. The familiar opening verses start this way:

The Lord is my shepherd, I shall not want.
He makes me lie down in green pastures;
he leads me beside still waters;
he restores my soul.

At a funeral Mass, special prayers are included for the person who has died. These are found in the Prayer of the Faithful and in the Commendation, when the priest "commends" the person into God's care.

15

Why do we end our prayers with "Amen"?

Saying "Amen" at the end of our prayers is a way of saying to God, "So be it" or "Yes, I believe in what I just said." We are saying that what we have heard in prayer coming from our own lips (or someone else's, if they are leading the prayer) is true.

"Amen" is an ancient word that is found in many different languages. It is in the Hebrew (Jewish) scriptures, became part of ancient Greek, and then was adopted into Latin by the Romans. From there it became part of English, French, Spanish, Italian and many other languages.

"Amen" is used by Catholic, *Protestant* and Orthodox Christians, and by Jewish worshippers. It is also found in some Muslim prayers.

PERSONAL WAYS OF PRAYING

16

Can we use our own words when we pray?

Yes! We are encouraged to pray to God using our own words. After all, these words are the best ones to tell God our deepest thoughts and feelings. Prayers in our own words could be brief thanks or words of praise, or may be more detailed descriptions of our worries or questions.

Another good thing about this prayer form is that you can use it anytime, anywhere. You do not need to memorize something or use a book to remind yourself what to say. All you need is the desire to have a conversation with God. Remember that if it is truly to be a conversation, you must also listen to God.

Sometimes you can prepare a prayer in your own words for a special occasion. You might be asked to lead *Grace* or class prayer, for example. You can combine your own words with a traditional prayer, such as the Our Father (the Lord's Prayer), if you like.

Another prayer method also uses short phrases. You can repeat a word or phrase over and over to help you concentrate. The Jesus Prayer repeats the phrase "Lord Jesus, have mercy on me, a sinner," or even "Jesus, mercy."

17

Is singing hymns a form of prayer?

St. Augustine would certainly agree. He wrote that to sing is to pray twice – through the words and through the music. Actually, we communicate in many ways when we sing.

When we sing hymns, we are singing our prayers to God. Often these are songs of praise, thanksgiving or trust. The words themselves form a prayer.

We are also singing a beautiful melody. Through music, we try to reflect back to God some of the beauty of creation. Sometimes our voices are not perfect, but when we sing together, many of these imperfections are covered up. People have different types of voices. When they blend together in harmony, we are telling God we can work together.

Singing solo or in a choir is also a way of serving other people and leading them into prayer through music. God has given each of us many gifts. It is up to us to share these gifts with the community.

Sometimes we forget why we are singing hymns. Next time you sing a hymn, remember that making sacred music is about communicating with God.

- Famous musicians in the Bible include Miriam, the sister of Moses, who played the tambourine, and David, who played the harp to calm King Saul.

- St. Cecilia is the patron saint of musicians.

- The Church has been a major force in the history of music. Christianity gave us Gregorian chant, Masses by Bach, Mozart and Beethoven, many versions of the Ave Maria, and other important works and musical techniques. Check out some of these types of music for yourself on the Internet, and share your favourites with your family or friends.

18

How can reading be prayer?

Think about the different reasons why we read. Sometimes we read for pleasure or to find information. But we can also read because we are looking for wisdom that only God can provide. At times like those, we turn to the Bible and the writings of holy men and women who have also searched for God. When we can feel or understand God's presence in the reading, then yes, it can indeed lead us to prayer.

When we read the Bible, we can feel God's presence in the sacred words. This presence is very clear in the Gospels. St. Ignatius of Loyola encouraged us to imagine ourselves as part of the action when we read a passage from scripture. Next time you read a Gospel story, imagine that you were there. Which character were you? What did you see or hear or feel? Then ask yourself what this passage has to do with your life today. Finally, ask what God is saying to you through this passage.

Reading certain types of books and poetry can lead us into prayer, too. We can find God's presence in stories of the triumph of good over evil or in the beauty of the flow of the words. This reading becomes prayer when we ask ourselves how God is found in this book. In the same way, some movies and plays can be a form of prayer. Seeing God in these works takes wisdom, because the sacred message is often hidden. It can help to talk about your ideas with your family, teachers and friends to explore your insights.

- Reading about the lives of saints and other holy people can inspire us. An excellent starting point is to look at the life of St. Francis of Assisi, St. Marguerite D'Youville, or Blessed Mother Teresa of Calcutta. One place to learn about these amazing people is in *25 Questions about Catholic Saints and Heroes.*

- Viewing great paintings or sculpture can also be a prayerful experience. Begin by praying with Sassoferrato's *Virgin at Prayer* and Caravaggio's *Supper at Emmaus.* You can easily find these images online.

19

How can writing be prayer?

Because writing is a form of communication, it can be a powerful form of prayer for some people. Writing your thoughts and feelings about your life and your relationship with God and others in a prayer journal is a great way to express yourself. (A prayer journal can be a notebook, a special blank book, or even a computer file.) You can spend time reading over what you have written and develop your ideas further, if you like. Writing down your prayerful thoughts will help you to know yourself better. You can ask yourself, Do I really mean that? Why did I write that? How is God responding to this prayer? In this way, your writing can lead you to deeper prayer.

Keeping a record of your prayers and thoughts in a journal can help you in other ways, too:

- You can see patterns or themes in your writing. If you see the same concerns arising often, you can ask trusted adults about them.
- You can see how your concerns have changed over time.
- You can share them with people you know. These words may inspire or comfort others and can let others know what you are feeling.

You might want to write in your prayer journal in the evening, as you look back on your day. You can give thanks to God for the good things and even for challenging moments that the day brought you. You can express your feelings about particular concerns and ask for God's help. You can use Bible passages as a starting point, writing down what God is saying to you in scripture. You can even write about books, movies, TV shows or music to discover any wisdom they might offer you for your life.

- St. Thérèse of Lisieux kept a journal of the thoughts she addressed to God. She used many of these words and prayers when she wrote her autobiography, *The Story of a Soul*. Her book became a bestseller!

- If you want to use scripture, experiences or the media to help you pray, here are some questions to guide you:

  - What happened?
  - How is God speaking to me in this experience?
  - How will I try to act or think differently from now on?

Then, close with a prayer of thanksgiving to God.

20

How can creating something be prayer?

The act of creating art or music or a craft can be a form of communication with God. In this sense, we can see it as a prayer.

God is the creator of life and ultimately, everything in the world. Any creative act is a gift back to God. This means that if we like to draw or paint or sculpt, we can turn our art into a prayer. We may want to tell God how we feel or we may want to give thanks. We can describe through our art the awe and wonder we have for creation.

Looking at a work of art, listening to music, or watching a movie or other performance can also be a form of prayer, if we look at how God is talking to us through these works. Being in nature can also be a prayerful experience. When we are in a beautiful setting, we can feel very close to God.

- Other activities such as acting, dancing, painting, gardening and building could be forms of creative prayer. Creating a website or blog could also be prayerful.
- This kind of prayer is sometimes called a prayer of expression.

21

Why is silence an important part of prayer?

We live in a noise-filled world. When is the last time you heard absolutely nothing? There always seems to be some noise trying to get our attention. But if we want to listen to God as part of our prayer, it helps to be in a place where we find stillness. We can often find that peace in a church, in our room or in nature.

The idea of finding a quiet place where we can meet God comes from scripture. The prophet Elijah is told that he will meet God on a mountain. There, Elijah experiences thunder, an earthquake and a roaring wind, but God is not found in these dramatic events. Finally, Elijah finds God in "a sound of sheer silence." (1 Kings 19:12) In Psalm 46 God says, "Be still, and know that I am God." We also have the example of Jesus, who often went off to a quiet place to pray. Quiet prayer is important to monks and nuns, who set aside hours for *meditation* each day.

In recent years, some people have turned to monks and nuns to learn how to meditate in this way. Many people find that this "centering" prayer helps them to be close to God.

The method is very simple.

- Find a quiet, comfortable place where you won't be disturbed or fall asleep. (It is best to sit rather than lie down to avoid getting sleepy.)
- To focus your mind, recite a short prayer phrase over and over in your head. You can use the Jesus Prayer (see Question 16) or the word *ma-ra-na-tha*. This is a word in Aramaic (the language Jesus spoke) that means "Come, Lord Jesus."
- Pray quietly for as long as you feel able: 5, 10, 15 or 20 minutes. If your mind wanders, just return to your prayer word.
- Finish by praying the Our Father or another prayer to God.

You can do this meditation by yourself or with your family or some friends.

Christian meditation is an ancient prayer practice of the Church that goes back to the fourth century.

Silent prayer is also an important part of Buddhist meditation. Some Buddhists try to empty their minds through sitting meditation called *zazen*.

Hindu writers describe our distracting thoughts as the sound of chattering monkeys. Some people recommend using a repeated phrase called a *mantra* to focus the mind. "Lord Jesus, have mercy on me, a sinner" is a mantra that is used in Christian meditation.

22

Why do we memorize certain prayers?

When we were younger, many of us learned a number of prayers by heart, such as the Sign of the Cross, Our Father, Glory Be and Hail Mary. Once we have memorized these prayers, we can pray them anytime or anywhere, and we can think about what they mean. After all, prayers are much more than words to memorize. They keep us in touch with God. The more we understand these phrases that connect us to God, the deeper our relationship with God will be. The more prayers we know, the more we have to help us deepen that relationship.

For 2,000 years, people have been praying to God through Jesus, Mary and the saints using memorized prayers. In a world without computers, where many people could not read and books were rare, people had to learn prayers by heart. Knowing these prayers helped them to give thanks in times of celebration and to seek comfort in times of sadness. When we say a Hail Mary, we are praying the same prayer that was prayed by a farmer plowing his field in Egypt 1,500 years ago, by a seamstress sewing clothes in Spain 1,000 years ago, and by settlers in New France 300 years ago.

We can pray these prayers in different ways, such as when we join with others in common prayer, or when our own words for prayer won't come. We can teach these prayers to a younger sister or brother, or to a friend. See the end of this book for the words to some well-known prayers you may want to memorize. Even today, when it is easy to find prayers in print and online, it is a good idea to learn some of your favourite ones by heart, so you can say them whenever you like.

Some people memorize passages from the Bible. Consider memorizing the Ten Commandments (Exodus 20: 1-17); Psalm 23 (The Lord is my shepherd); the Beatitudes (Matthew 5:3-12); and Luke 4:16-21.

23

Do we pray to change God's mind?

Sometimes we think we can bargain with God. Our prayer might go something like this: "God, if I am a really good person and help out at home and do all my homework, then can I grow taller than my brother?" If our prayer follows this pattern, then we have to rethink how we pray and how we understand God. God is not a cosmic magician. God knows our deepest desires and thoughts. We pray to bring God into our own mind. When we pray, we try to get as close to God's ways of thinking as we can. Jesus is the way to God's mind and heart. Ending our prayers with the words "through Jesus Christ our Lord" shows the close or intimate connection between Jesus and God.

We pray to have the courage of Christ to deal with our challenges. We pray to have the wisdom of Christ to face our sorrows and joys. We pray to have the faith of Christ when doubts cast shadows over our hearts. We pray to have the hope of Christ when we look to the future, with all its uncertainties. And we pray to have the love of Christ to deepen our friendships.

So we don't pray to change God's mind, we pray to change *our* minds. By becoming more like Christ, we become true sons and daughters of God and we live as Christ has shown us.

Soren Kierkegaard, a Danish philosopher and theologian, wrote, "Prayer does not change God, but it changes [the one] who prays."

24

Does God always answer our prayers?

Sometimes we pray to God for a miracle. We haven't studied as much as we should, so we ask God for help on a test. But nothing seems to happen. We still don't do well on the test. We pray for someone we love to recover from a serious illness, but they die anyway. Where was God? we might wonder. Why weren't our prayers answered? God does answer our prayers, but not necessarily in a way that we expect. There are a few things to keep in mind about how God answers prayers.

God knows what we want even before we ask it. You may pray for success on a test, but may not have noticed that you have already had many opportunities to learn the material: by paying attention in class, doing homework, and following a study plan for review. God isn't a wizard who grants wishes. God asks us to do our part to achieve our goals. In the case of serious illness, God has given us the tools and ability to heal many people and prevent others from getting sick. But death is a part of the human condition. We pray to make the ending of life a loving and sacred time.

When we put ourselves in a difficult situation, God is with us, even suffering with us, but God cannot take away our free will, which was to do other things rather than preparing for a test.

Sometimes the best thing that can happen in the long run is for us to fail in the short run. If we do poorly on a test because we did not study well, then we learn that our actions have consequences. Learning from our errors can help us to become stronger.

We cannot always hear God's voice answering our prayers because we are distracted. Our lives are busy and noisy. We need to listen and watch for signs of God in our lives. When we take time to listen, we can hear God's answer to our prayers more clearly.

Frederick Douglass, an escaped slave, once said, "I prayed for 20 years but received no answer until I prayed with my legs." What do you think he meant?

25

How does prayer help the world?

When we pray, we aren't making anything you can touch or feeding the hungry. So what's the point? Is there any practical use for prayer? The answer is yes! Prayer helps us to heal our damaged world. Prayer draws us closer to God, who wants us to go out into the world and make it whole and beautiful. In other words, God gives us inspiration in prayer so we do acts of justice and love for others.

Many great men and women, including St. Francis of Assisi, St. Vincent de Paul, Mahatma Gandhi, Martin Luther King Jr. and Blessed Mother Teresa, depended on a deep prayer life to help them in their work with the poor, the outcast and the hungry. Prayer is the spiritual food that gives us strength to do the right thing in the face of injustice.

Prayer helps us to help others. When we pray for other people, we are letting God know that we are concerned about those who need special care.

Prayer brings balance and hope to our own lives, too. We are busy people who have many different activities: school, sports, hobbies or just hanging out with friends. There is also time with family and time for relaxing. We can get so busy doing things, we lose track of our meaning and purpose in life. Setting aside time to be with God in prayer helps us remember what is important in life.

St. Josemaria Escriva wrote, "To pray is to talk to God, but about what? About Him, about yourself; joys, sorrows, successes, and failures, noble ambitions, daily worries, weaknesses! And acts of thanksgiving and petitions: and Love and reparation. In a word: to get to know Him and to get to know yourself: to get acquainted."

WORDS TO KNOW

Abba: The Aramaic word that Jesus used in his prayer to God. It means "Father."

Adoration: Honouring and loving God in prayer.

Aramaic: The language that Jesus spoke. He also read Hebrew.

Blessing: God's good will.

Breviary: A book that contains a form of prayer called the Liturgy of the Hours.

Divine Office: Another name for the Liturgy of the Hours.

Gospels: The four books of the Bible that tell the Good News of Jesus Christ. They are the Gospels of Matthew, Mark, Luke and John.

Grace: A prayer that is often used at mealtimes. It also means God's eternal love for us.

Intercession: A prayer asking for God's help.

Kyrie: The hymn we sing early in the Mass asking God to have mercy on us.

Magnificat: Mary's prayer of praise to God, found in the first chapter of Luke's Gospel.

Mantra: A phrase or word that people repeat silently while meditating, to help them focus their minds in prayer.

Meditation: A form of silent prayer.

Petition: A prayer made in the form of a request.

Protestants: A branch of Christianity that began about 500 years ago. Some Protestant churches in Canada include the United Church, the Presbyterian Church and the Lutheran Church.

Psalms: Sacred songs. The Bible contains 150 psalms. We sing or read a psalm at Mass.

Sacrament: A visible sign and action of God's love. There are seven sacraments in the Catholic Church: Baptism, Confirmation, Eucharist, Reconciliation (Penance), Holy Orders (for men being ordained as deacons, priests and bishops), Marriage, and Anointing of the Sick.

The Sign of the Cross

In the name of the Father,
[using your right hand, touch your forehead]
and of the Son, [touch your chest]
and of the Holy Spirit.
[touch your left shoulder, then your right shoulder]
Amen.

Glory Be

Glory be to the Father,
and to the Son,
and to the Holy Spirit.
As it was in the beginning,
is now, and ever shall be,
world without end.
Amen.

The Lord's Prayer

Our Father, who art in heaven,
hallowed be thy name;
thy kingdom come;
thy will be done
on earth as it is in heaven.
Give us this day our daily bread;
and forgive us our trespasses
as we forgive those who trespass against us;
and lead us not into temptation,
but deliver us from evil.
Amen.